Into the Heart of
Our Humanity

Revised Edition

Mark Elder

Printed in the United States of America
Printed by CreateSpace

ISBN 978-0-9964499-2-2 (paperback)

Published by
Property of Humanity Press

Front Cover Image by
iStockphoto

Dedicated to
my sons,
Anthony and Steven,
the very best part of
the heart of my humanity.

"You do not have to be good.
You do not have to walk on your knees
for a hundred miles through the desert, repenting.
You only have to let the soft animal of your body
love what it loves."

Mary Oliver
from Wild Geese

Contents

Preface   ix

First Words   1

Our Being   7

Our Acceptance   21

Our Fulfillment   29

Our Loss   35

Our Longing   41

Our Hope   53

Our Expression   65

Our Struggle   75

Our Courage   83

Our Obligation   91

Last Words   99

About the Author   103

Preface

What is going on?

Humanity seems utterly broken.

Can we be fixed? I do not know. I will not try here, but I will suggest there is a much better way to perceive ourselves and each other.

I intend to explore who we are as humans and how that dramatically impacts our understanding and actions toward one another.

The time is now for such a movement as this. A movement to see our common human story. I believe many of you would agree we cannot waste time as we further drift apart.

I do not want a mere reading of this book, I want a pondering. I am sure you could read this book in one easy sitting. Let it go through the distillation process. This we must do unless the force of our busy lives keeps us from doing the work we need to do.

I have spent four years pondering these thoughts. I do not expect nor want a rush to acceptance and action. Over some period of time, I hope these words find a place to calmly enter into your experience.

Please take your time. Stop. Set the book down. Carry a thought with you. Argue and debate. Embrace and discard. Love or hate. Most of all I ask you to listen.

I have provided some help in the structure of the book. You can read one sentence and hopefully have a complete thought to reflect on, maybe scratch a note in the open spaces. Like life itself, so much is lived and understood in the space between tasks and tending. Hopefully, you will have this experience.

Now, to the gratitude I feel.

No one walks through life alone. No one writes alone either. The writer always has some witnesses peering in and cheering on the action. I am surrounded by many witnesses.

Dear patients and your families, mentors, friends, colleagues, strangers and loved ones, how do I say thank you? I will have to let the words of this book stand as my thanks. For in these words and verse is your voice and influence.

I would not know of humanity in the deeper parts if not for you all.

I would not know of courage had I not seen you live it.

I would not know what proper reverence for life looks like had I not had the chance to marvel you all model it.

Yes, you all have added to the voice of this book.

Your resolute lives, your wounded souls, your abiding hope and your willingness to let me move in close to you have wholly shaped me.

I can only hope this is an authentic outpouring of what we have seen and shared and who we are as strangers, friends and loved ones.

Gratitude flows from the deep.

First Words

We find our human story in a state of fury.

A growing impersonal social network is threatening to define us by reactions people have to a post.

We live in a world dense with activity and our lives are being overcome by the push.

We kill and wound each other too quickly.

We offer life and healing too slowly.

We solve our problems with less solemnity and civility.

We must look deeply into our lives and find the reverence for something more significant than our next post, or next scheduled activity, or next war, or next purchase, or next argument.

Breathe here. Consider with me, what is the great story being told by our humanity?

**

What story is being told between the lines and headlines of our lives?

What story is being told by the family defined in many ways yet all seeking love?

What story is being told by the wealthy, ravaged by fear of losing it all?

What story is being told by the artist who dares imagine beauty or brokenness for the world?

What story is being told by the single mother who holds her children wondering about their wellbeing?

What story is being told by the teenager with a defiant and dreamy stare into the future?

What story is being told by those who are so badly abused that life has long ceased to have value?

What story is being told by the aging widow?

What story is being told by the children at play?

What story is being told by the refugee?

Is there a common story about humanity that reveals the mystery and beauty of all the combined stories of our lives?

***

I hold the fundamental belief there is such a story and that by knowing the story we can understand our lives together.

Unless we can understand this story, our humanity will continue to slip from us and we will live our lives measured only by time and activity.

Unless we can understand this story, we will live as self-interested beings never fully knowing or seeing others we should be calling our brother or sister.

We need to recover this story for the sake of us remaining alive and fully living.

This is the fury of life we must face, reckoning with this story.

This is my pursuit.

This is the journey.

I hope it becomes all of ours.

Our Being

When we find ourselves at the edge of life where despair and death await and resolve to live on, to live one more moment, this is our desires prompting us to choose life.

When we surround ourselves in an experience for which there are no words, this is desire reminding us of the depth and mystery of our lives.

When emotion flows from our porous lives, this is desire erupting, unwilling to remain silent.

Our desires *are* our humanity.

Our desires *are* our primal nature of being in this world.

Our human story begins with desire.

We are not born of the sinner's heart first, hateful and angry.

We are born first with desire.

We desire for something or someone that assuages our restless and fearful moments.

We desire to gaze beyond where our shallow and blurry eyes are able to see.

We desire to feel comforted.

We desire to test the limits of our known world.

We desire to heal from wounds believed incurable.

We desire to embark on a thing thought impossible.

We deny death and disease every day because our desires guide us toward life.

***

All the activity,

all the growth,

all the progress,

all the pain,

all the sorrow,

all the joy,

all these,

all are markings, etched into our life,

all, energized by desire.

***

We have heard it said, "I think, therefore I am," let us re-imagine ourselves as,

I *desire*, therefore I am.

***

The greatest of all the universal wonders is our human desire.

Without desire, no human-made wonder comes into being, and no natural wonder is ever perceived as wonderful.

Without desire, mystery washes away and reveals a daily existence dependent on routine and patterns that leave us empty of wonder.

Without desire, love never meets lover.

Without desire, our cities are mere shelter and not beloved places of belonging.

Without desire, our thoughts are stale and never promote exploration and learning.

Without desire, our hope for a future story remains but an empty page.

Without desire, there is little purpose to all our actions.

Without desire, the music of "An Ode to Joy" is but noise that perhaps never comes into existence at all.

Without desire, our work has no reason.

Without desire, we are resistant to creating new experiences and tolerate resignation.

***

Desire pours from us as water from a spring, from a pure place worthy of our tasting and we do.

The worthiness, dare it be said, the holiness of our desire has been under siege for millennia of righteous fire meant to destroy our desire and replace it with shame and guilt.

Desire as sin yells at us that we are flawed in need of salvation.

Desire as the source of pain asks us to detach from it in order to obtain enlightened peace.

Desire as mere pleasure complains we are beings only in search of self-gratification.

Surely, a new story of desire must be told and embraced.

Desire sustains us through the pain.

Desire transforms looking at the stars or some ocean view into a rapturous moment of exultation.

Desire opens us up to a universe of discovery.

Desire leads us to those we love, places we belong, things to which we attach.

Desire gives cause to our work.

Desire provides aim to our life.

Desire composes stories of the unknown and these myths sustain us when reality is just too hard, too well known.

Desire is dream-making and dream-living.

Desire and their fulfillment is our wellbeing.

Desire is the soul and the spirit of the human...**Every. Single. Human.**

***

Seven Noble Desires animate our humanity.

Desire for Health—

We desire our body, mind and spirit to be well, not perfectly so, but healthy enough to move toward our fullest life.

This movement forward, toward our fullest life, is the experience of our vitality.

Vitality is the necessary energy we need to move toward all other desire.

Desire for Self-Determination—

We desire freedom to map for ourselves the path our life will take.

No freedom is absolute as it is bound by civility and law, nature and random cause, but all freedom is resolute in its desire for a life that is not extinguished by suffocating control.

Desire for Pleasure—

We desire the sensual not just for mere entertainment, but also meaningful and lasting joy.

We long to see the beautiful, hear the rhythmic, smell the lovely, feel the lover, and taste the savory.

Every day the desire for pleasure pulsates within us waiting for and experiencing delight.

Desire for Belonging—

We desire a connection to people, places and things. A connection that roots us in the world from which we receive love and companionship and the daily reminder we are not alone.

We all belong to this earth and vast universe, and our challenge is to live in good stewardship of what we are fortunate to have and hold.

The good stewardship of belonging drives our compassion and love outward toward others.

Desire for belonging prompts us to *"do unto others as we would have them do unto you."*

Desire for Exploration—

Something amazing awaits us just around the corner or in some unknown place.

Who will go and search it out?

"We will!" is our resounding response because our desire to know and explore would have it no other way.

Our curiosity takes us there.

Our curiosity imagines the journey to get there.

Our quest to understand leads us to the bold questions, "What happens next?" "What is yet to be known?"

Our small lives are made larger when we expand our mind and hearts with exploration and never give up on learning a new thing.

Desire for Achievement—

We desire a life of significance.

We desire that our effort is worth the doing, and that all the toil and tears worth the being.

When we die we desire to leave something of ourselves to this world, something everlasting…a legacy of life lived well.

Desire for Faith—

Our desire for faith is the human experience of trust.

Our need for trust searches heaven and earth for sources worthy of our trust, and when found, desire for faith explodes in profound reverence.

The desire for faith must accept our doubt, for the world is unsettled and faith must thrive during a crisis of trust, when the willingness to forsake all desire rises strong.

***

Seven desires form the DNA of our humanity.

Seven desires proclaim, "This is who you are." "This is the foundation of your story."

Seven desires that constitute our human soul and spirit.

Seven desires that make all humans spiritual creatures alive with wonder.

Seven desires, *the heart of our humanity.*

Breathe here. Take this in.

Our Acceptance

Our seven desires come natural but they are not naturally lived with ease.

They become infinitely harder when we perceive them only as demanding and that which brings us pain.

If desire for achievement is only lived as the demand for getting things done, as work without a purpose behind them, then desire will feel regimented.

If desire for faith is practiced as belief and command only, then faith does not move toward the trust but toward practices that keep faith bound by finite expectations of results. Faith is the absolute journey in mystery where no expectation can be found.

If desire for self-determination is dedicated to the pursuit of selfish-determination to the exclusion or apathy of others determining for themselves a path in life, then in all cases the denouncement of the self is achieved.

If desire for exploration is only expressed in what can be achieved with no risk attached, then our lives walk in fear to be ignited by possibility.

If desire for belonging is experienced as a demand to love or be loved then belonging converts to possession and nurture is not expressed but rather extracted.

If desire for health is lived as fear of disease, death and destruction then vitality seeps from us and we are left to our vices in overcoming our fear.

If desire for pleasure is engulfed by the demand for purity of the experience then pleasure is lived in the shadows and subconscious where only punishable offenses of self-gratification exists.

We begin to curse our desires believing they set us up for disappointment, but we are deeply driven by them.

We distance ourselves from desires believing salvation and peace come in separation from them, and then go on to live hidden lives of guilt and shame, lives of *"quiet desperation."*

We take other paths of convenience to pacify ourselves, ignoring our deepest desires.

Our desires lead us to our true self and in finding our true self we discover our longed for meaning.

***

Perhaps it is time to say, "No!" to the scheme that keeps our lives in submission to fear.

Say no, to more messages that confuse our humanity with nightmarish tales of condemnation and meaninglessness.

Say no, to mere activity divorced from desire that swallows more time and spits out less life.

Say no, to interrupted time, and search instead for unbroken moments that allow desire to vibrate in us.

Say no, to the temptation of denying ourselves and each other the whole experience of desire.

Say no, to the tyranny of our modern rushed lives.

Say no, to seeing without observation.

Say no, to hearing without listening.

Say no, to tasting without savoring.

Say no, to touching without feeling.

Say no, to doing without being.

If we let the fullness of desires deeply root within us, then our story is attached to authenticity.

***

Then, we can say "Yes!"

Say yes, to pleasure and know it is birthed from a natural place and not extracted from us only to be called evil.

Say yes, to a life that moves away from entitlement to gratification and enforcing our own way, and toward a life of generosity.

Say yes, to the bold assertion of our achievement and pass it on for the good of humanity and as something everlasting.

Say yes, to curiosity and the mysteries that await our discovery.

Say yes, to loving even at the risk of losing,

Say yes, to taking care of the only life we have, and taking care of the lives and world entrusted to us.

Say yes, to a faith that searches for trusted sources of hope and meaning, and when found holds them not as a source of power and control, but in humility and gratefulness.

Say yes, to being AND doing, each finding their place within the unfolding moments of our lives.

Say yes, to desires, in reverence for what they are and mean to us.

Acceptance of our desires is work and a life-long journey to understand and embrace but we can start now.

Our Fulfillment

From the earliest days of our existence to our last, we are driven to fulfill desire. Each moment, longing for one more experience with our desires.

One more chance to see the sunset burning its last light of day.

One more act of love with our lovely.

One more prayer offered in faith.

One more sharing of heart-felt words.

These are the moments we live for, moments that remind us how special our lives are.

Moments when we have sight of new life.

Moments when freedom's voice breaks forth in bold sound.

Moments of embrace from a friend.

Moments when the night sky overwhelm us with more infinity than we can fathom.

We are fulfilled when life comes together for us in acts of achievement; when our acts define our capacity to fully live.

Acts that provide another story toward legacy.

Acts that use creativity to produce the astonishing.

Acts that take us to the places of our dreams.

Acts that help us reach a goal.

Our lives become rich from the simple.

The simple refreshing from water.

The simple pleasure of touch.

The simple show of kindness.

The simple belief in the good existing in all forms of life.

We are fulfilled when we take steps to enhance life.

Take steps toward healing.

Take steps toward courageous acts of survival.

Take steps to redeem what is broken.

Take steps that embrace strength.

Fulfillment comes in many ways and it produces a sound as we celebrate.

Laughter bursts from us.

Clapping applauds that which we love.

Music moves us to sing and dance.

Cries of joy move us deeper into our life.

Yes, we pursue the fulfillment of our desires, each one of us, every day.

Our bodies rise to meet a new day because desire rises, calling us forward in action to make and have for ourselves, and hopefully others, a life of fulfillment.

Fulfillment of desires is not devoid of risk.

This we all know.

Our Loss

Being human is hard.

Fulfillment comes and then it goes.

Our desires are kept no secret from pain.

The pain is from the loss.

Our desires are beaten from us.

Our desires get blown away, gone in an instant.

Our desires are broken beyond repair.

Our desires are stripped from us leaving us exposed and in search of shelter.

Our desires render us vulnerable to loss.

Loss has an infinite array in which it can attack us.

We lose touch with friends.

We lose a sense of perspective.

We lose hope.

We lose concern for others.

We lose time.

Do we know our losses?

We lose loved ones.

We lose our way.

We lose our health.

We lose our work.

We lose clean air.

Have we dealt with the pain of loss?

We lose water to drink and grow.

We lose our connections.

We lose our abilities.

We lose trust.

We lose faith in others.

Are we willing to accept moving on in life with loss?

We lose faith in a god, in transcendence.

We lose innocence.

We lose our identity.

We lose a baby.

We lose the means to keep ourselves alive.

What will our losses teach us and help us to become?

We lose something of ourselves and our world each second of each hour of every day.

Loss ushers in the undeniable presence of pain.

Loss lingers in its natural state of grief.

Loss is a river through our lives carrying away bits and pieces of who we are.

Our attempts to stop loss are noble and natural and best viewed as courageous acts not as victorious conquering.

No thing or one is permanent.

We borrow our days from the reality of loss.

Loss is with us and our language and life must reflect its existence, lest we slip into denial and live only to have and hold but never wanting or knowing how to love and let go.

This must be said, our lives are forever better and changed when we acquaint ourselves with and feel ALL our losses well.

Our Longing

Our human nature strives for the fulfillment of our desires, yet loss perpetuates a continual need for replenishment.

This endless cycle of gaining and losing is both the blessing and battle of our lives.

Desire lived in this cycle of having and losing becomes our journey of longing.

Without longing we do not seek fulfillment nor risk loss.

If we neither seek nor risk, we cannot find a life of meaning.

If we do not find meaning, then our desires die in the clinched teeth of apathy.

We need our longing to push us toward our desire.

***

When the party is over,

When the silence moves in,

When all we have to listen to is our own voice,

When we are finished with the last task,

Longing tells us we are not complete.

Longing stays to keep the pulse of desire strong.

When the friend moves away,

When the faithful depart from the places of prayer,

When the snow melts from the last peak,

When we manage all the changes,

Longing keeps us honest.

Longing carries us through unimaginable loss.

When the problem is unsolved,

When the search for meaning goes on,

When we love as much as we can,

When we wonder at the beautiful,

Longing befriends our anxiety.

Longing helps us to imagine in the dark.

When we have strived in competition,

When we have tasted of all savory things,

When we fear the loss of life,

When we work as hard as our bodies will allow,

Longing drives us for more.

Longing looks into the distance.

When we feel our wounds,

When all the money has been spent,

When the bombs have torn down the cities,

When our privilege has been won at the expense of others,

Longing reminds us that to be fully alive is not easy.

Longing becomes our voice when words fail.

When we search for happiness in everything that shines,

When sickness moves in,

When all things have been bought up,

When youth succumbs to aging,

Longing leaves us uneasy.

Longing is a path, sometimes the only one.

When we rise to a new day,

When we rest at the end of the day,

When we reflect at the end of another year,

When we reach the end of our life,

Longing continues its life within us.

In the final beat of our heart, longing will pump through our veins.

The truth of our living is that our longing cannot be silenced or stilled.

***

Longing lives in the gaps, in the gaps between our having and having not.

We have understood and we have not.

We have loved and we have not.

We have had dreams fulfilled and we have not.

We have had our health and we have not.

Breathe here, in the gap.

We have felt connected in this world and we have not.

We have known laughter and we have not.

We have had the security of a job and we have not.

We have had all we wanted and we have not.

Sit still here, in the gap.

We have experienced justice and we have not.

We have used time wisely and we have not.

We have been self-absorbed and we have not.

We have believed in God and we have not.

Honor the process of longing here, in the gap.

We have had answers and we have not.

We have opened our eyes to the world and we have not.

We are proud of some things we have done and others we are not.

We have helped others and we have not.

Find ways of healing here, in the gap.

We have leaned toward kindness and we have not.

We have felt safe and we have not.

We have used our courage for good and we have not.

We have our life today and one day we will not.

Develop your strength here, in the gap.

Our strength is tested by questions that grow here, in the gap.

***

We wonder if we will be okay?

Why has this happened to me?

Where is the good?

Will my good life be taken from me?

Why am I so fortunate and others so cruelly
punished?

When will I feel happy again?

What is wrong with me?

Who am I?

When will the world be healed?

What is my future?

Will I lose all that I cherish?

Will those I love be able to live well?

Will I find food and water today?

Who will love me?

Is this the day I, or someone I love, dies?

Then, just when we believe we have answers or grow comfortable in our existence, life turns, and again we have not.

We are left with longing.

We are restless.

Our longing leads us to search for fulfillment.

***

We search in the course of our busy lives.

We search in markets full of merchandise.

We search in hallowed halls of education.

We search in holy places of worship.

We search in forbidden pleasures.

We search in our history.

We search the wonders of beauty.

We search in our work.

We search among the words.

We search in the table of food before us.

We search in our loves.

We search in the secret places.

We search everywhere.

Longing lives in us as surely as we breathe.

As surely as we breathe, our longing will be.

Our Hope

Longing drives us to search and our hope leads us to rest.

Let the fervor of our longing be matched by the calming assurance of our hope.

***

We hope beyond the searching and striving of each day.

We hope our desires will lead us to healing and not tear us down in weakness.

We hope our losses do not overwhelm us.

We hope fulfillment comes in healing waves of contentment.

We hope our longing serves as the gift that keeps us guided toward the better parts of our life.

We hope our faith will rest in trust and that our trust is rooted in what is real.

We hope for living well through each dying moment.

We hope for tomorrow's return.

We hope in beauty that lifts us to imagine a different and better world.

We hope that our wounded body, mind and soul will mend.

We hope water will be found to sustain our thirsty cells.

We hope pleasure reveals itself in simple moments of restorative satisfaction.

We hope in the buoyance of joy.

We hope fear will not freeze us to inaction.

We hope the plans we make find their way to completion.

We hope in a neighbor being ready to help in our time of need.

We hope to be that neighbor for someone.

We hope pleasure will come even as our senses dull and age.

We hope our life leaves a whisper that echoes when we are gone.

We hope, because not to is certain despair.

***

Hope can be unsettling.

Hope is unsettling because it must thrive in the fog of the unknown.

Hope is unsettling because it calls us to truthfully engage who we are and what we want to become.

Hope is unsettling because it is not fantasy.

Hope is unsettling because the resistance on the surface of our lives is immense to abandon hope and live for what we can see and possess in the unsettled now.

Hope is unsettling because our energy is drained by activity leaving us precious little time and patience to experience hope.

Whatever is unsettling, we must let hope move us on.

We need to move on toward embracing our desire, feeling blessed by their life-giving impulses.

We need to move on toward fulfillment of our desire for the good, casting aside the hurtful, and experience fulfillment as an opportunity to both give and receive.

We need to move on through the valley of the shadow of loss with the hope of healing and restoration.

We need to move on toward the contentment that hope provides.

***

Contentment accepts the gap between our having and having not.

Contentment keeps the engine of desire burning without burning out.

Contentment relaxes in the presence of enough and moderates the impulse to grab for more.

Contentment understands life is difficult and does not grow bitter in defeat; strength is increased with such wisdom.

Contentment can listen, then listens more, then understands, then responds in authentic reflection.

Contentment does not view change and loss as a reason for hope to disappear but as an opportunity for courage to rise.

Contentment is not a status achieved but a state of being experienced.

Contentment is gained not only by winning and good fortune, it thrives in hardship.

Contentment is knowing someone is helped by your life, that your effort makes a difference to them.

Contentment walks with longing, patiently waiting and paying attention to its process of searching.

Contentment sees longing as our companion and not as an enemy meant to scare, shame, and demolish our life.

Contentment is the gift of seeing no color, no creed, no religion and seeing the connection to the common story of all humanity.

Contentment is the healing that comes after loss, healing that is more than momentary appeasement of pain, but a sustainable force of good in us.

Contentment can live and let go, not in fear, but in the reality nothing is held forever.

Possess and let go.

Experience and let go.

Work and let go.

Try and let go.

Win and let go.

Love and let go.

Desire and let go.

Let go of the lust of desire.

Let go of the lust for power.

Let go of the lust to win at all cost.

Let go of the lust for possession.

Contentment rises when our lives unclench and unwind and our desires become a beautiful way to live and not a weapon to wound.

Contentment is the meaning we seek in our lives.

Why?

Contentment allows the light of hope into the dark places.

Contentment connects life to the grand narrative of humanity.

Contentment observes the smallest of things and transforms them into big meaning.

Contentment is open to the presence of others sharing our beautiful story together.

Contentment carries both wins and wounds in balance.

Contentment is a disciplined mind that grows wise with reason and moved by feeling.

Contentment embodies a spirit of desire with grace and kindness.

Contentment lives authentically and not falsely in a story made of contrived and forced scripts.

Contentment lives within the bounds of enough.

We hope for contentment.

In contentment, our search for meaning rests.

This is our hope.

Our Expression

The story is so vast that lives in the heart of humanity through all our desire, our loss, our fulfillment, our longing and our hope.

The story demands liberation from our interior lives and bold expression to the world.

In millions of ways, through the lives of billions of humans, over the course of thousands of years our human story is told.

The languages we speak,

The places we visit,

The people we love,

The houses we build,

The books we read and write,

The food we prepare,

The music we dance to,

The communities we foster,

The gods we worship,

The clothes we wear,

The emotions that leave us exposed,

Only the universe, with its billions of galaxies, can parallel the vastness of our diversity and the expression of our story.

***

We are the painters who colorfully brush our world and lives, revealing the sensual and beautiful.

We are the musicians who put language and note together and give our story a beat, a melody, a sound for all the brewing in us, both barbaric and refined.

We are the friends who sit in silence capturing the essence of another as they speak of their lives and then remain with them in the void.

We are the curious ever looking and listening for new and creative ways to learn and be surprised.

We are the beautiful and handsome waiting for our lover's approving gaze and touch.

We are explorers of an earth and universe too large for our minds, but not too grand for the exercising of our desires.

We are the consumers of food and drink that gather at the table or upon the mat, and the taste satisfies something deeper in our lives than mere hunger.

We are residents of places filled with history.

We are the emotional ones whose tears and laughter speak for us and the wide range of feelings reveal the depth of our story.

We are majestic and mythic storytellers creating a world of characters to be for us and with us when we cannot be or do for ourselves.

We are the wounded in search of healing, and ready to offer hand and heart to others who are wounded.

We are the worshipful; bending the knee in humility to pray and prostrate towards something beyond ourselves as a reminder that infinite mystery exceeds our finite mind.

We are the stylists who wear our personality as design making sure we are seen for who we are and what we feel.

We are the competitors who train our bodies to go into the arena and give our best, yes to win, but more importantly declare we showed up and gave our best effort.

We are the survivors who bend and break and then fix our eyes forward on life again.

We are the creators of new ideas.

We are the builders of bold spaces.

We are the searchers who peek behind, lift up, go into, forge across, ask something bold, seek something else, ever shaping our lives by that which we find interesting.

We are billions of humans revealing the deeper story of our humanity.

All this expression, all this diversity of expression, emanating from the same place in each of us.

In a hundred lifetimes we could never learn of all our diversity, but we can understand its common source.

Because this we know, at the end of our differences, resides a similar human story.

Our desires define us.

Our journey of fulfillment and through loss shapes us.

Our restless longing keeps us searching.

We all hope in something that pushes us forward toward meaning and contentment. We cannot remain silent and we do not.

We all express this life in amazing diversity, and our strength is in the commonality of our humanity.

We will reform our lives together when we become aware of this grand truth.

***

When we profane another, we profane ourselves.

When we judge another unworthy for who they are, we judge ourselves the same.

When we demand exclusivity of our way of life furthers our alienation from the human story.

When we hate the other, we hate ourselves.

When we believe truth is the property of only a few is a failure to understand the truth we all possess and live.

When a human shares an encounter with another and awareness and acceptance comes of the commonality of their humanity, this meeting becomes the healing force for the world.

Breathe here. Trust this encounter.

***

We are naive in our understanding of this fundamental truth of our human story.

Our naiveté about our common humanity comes with painful consequences.

We continue our killing because differences are believed to be the powerful source of evil.

We continue to shut the door of hospitality.

We continue to abort goo dialogue.

We continue to turn a vengeful eye toward the world and each other.

We continue to grow smaller in our mind about the vastness and goodness of humanity.

We continue to see the expressions of our common story as only cultural and local, not as an epic story of humanity unfolding.

We continue to foster fear as we look at each other with terror-filled eyes.

This we must do now…

We need not let our diversity of expression hinder us from seeing the deep story we share.

Join in the chorus of Namaste…blessed is the sacred story of humanity that is in you that is also in all of us.

Our Struggle

This human journey, this amazing story is expressed in infinite ways before us by the vast humanity around us.

Our story has a beauty and depth of soul unmatched by any other creature or thing on earth or in heaven.

The end?

No, there are uncomfortable things to talk about.

Our story is daunted by struggle.

Our story is visited by the pain of being alive.

***

Anxiety—

Rises when loss separates us from our desires.

Confronts us when desires are not understood.

Anxiety—

Increases as our capacity to fulfill desires slips from us.

Judges what is lacking as unworthy of value.

Anxiety—

Misses the deep current of our desires as the noise on the surface distracts us.

Grabs and clamors for satisfaction and attaches little meaning to the moment.

Rushes for fulfillment, impatient in longing.

Anxiety—

Consumes and possesses over and above all else and lives a destructive narrative that forces a status in life that is bought and always in peril of losing.

Equates fulfillment with wealth.

Anxiety—

Overwhelms our emotions and can turn them into disconnected feelings and destructive forces of rage and aggression.

Worries that hope will not be able to guide through the dread of our days toward contentment.

Anxiety—

Demands control.

Labels everyone and everything and is unable and unwilling to live in the openness of life.

Anxiety—

Toils under the false demands and denunciation of desire.

Feels disconnected even when life is in abundance all around.

Anxiety—

Overcompensates in activity for the missing elements in life and the breeding of addiction is at risk.

Depresses and stresses life and puts us in pain.

Anxiety—

Removes reason from decision.

Insists dis-ease is the reality of life.

***

Suffering—

Anxiety that is unmanaged and unrelenting.

***

Despair—

Suffering that abides.

***

These are our struggles and we do not end life without an encounter with them.

These are our struggles and we should not go through life pretending we are neither stunned nor traumatized by them.

These are our struggles, they are the *"dark night of the soul."*

These are our struggles and far better for us to manage them and allow the light of other parts of the human story to inform the darkness.

These are our struggles and we should take great care to amend our path lest we only come to live beleaguered lives.

These are our struggles, and yet, our story does not end nor should it end here.

Our Courage

We live on amid our struggles, even overcome them, with the courage we possess.

The only path to a life sustained and a life of wholeness is the path marked by courage.

We must seek courage in all moments, even when it seems as though it will not be found; courage searches in the dark.

Our human story depends on courage.

Without courage our desires become cause to live without reason to give.

Without courage our losses become too insurmountable.

Without courage our fulfillment becomes narrowly focused on ourselves.

Without courage our longing crushes our soul in the search for meaning.

Without courage we damage each other.

Without courage we grow anxious wondering about our strength and capacity to rise.

Without courage anxiety grows and our suffering looms.

Without courage life is a slow march to despair.

Yet, we have all managed, by our courage, to live to see this day in our life.

Courage pulses deep inside calling us to somewhere, to something, to be someone we are not, yet.

Courage is the foundation to our finding desire again amid our losses.

Courage channels fear into purposeful activity.

Courage confronts the questions and wills us to live on with them, even if unanswered.

Courage is our moral and spiritual impulse that points us toward contentment and not just mere survival.

Courage sees life within life, sees life within swirling death.

Courage stands when falling is suggested.

Courage renews when life is wounded.

Courage does not always result in winning, yet it always calls for our best effort to try.

Courage seeks help when resources are depleted.

Courage desires to heal not to harm.

Courage is memory willing to reconcile the past and its pain.

Courage attempts to mend what is broken.

Courage is hospitality to a stranger.

Courage is not loaded guns pointed at someone but loaded reason willing to solve the difficult questions.

Courage is faith comfortable with mystery.

Courage sees the world in unique wholeness.

Courage is our will-to-live in loss and our will-to-let-go when we are fulfilled enough.

Courage is our daily fuel to get up and face whatever may come.

Courage seeks a path through the hardship.

Courage lets go when holding on is too painful.

Courage sees loss not as life being unfair, but life being layered and complicated.

Courage is the willingness to expose our vulnerability to others for the sake of truth.

Courage moves us from behind the shield of excuses.

Courage is the vulnerability of love.

Courage is exploring the unknown.

Courage is trying even amid the fear of failure.

Courage is finding our own voice.

Courage is compromise.

Courage is seeing the other point of view.

Courage is listening to understand.

Courage is admitting when you have enough.

Courage is letting go of control, when control means harm.

Courage is seeing beyond the fearful present.

Courage is belief in a cause other than your own.

Courage keeps us alive in the midst of having nothing.

Courage returns color to the world through artful and mindful acts of observation.

Courage returns us back to our desires after loss.

Courage lets go when hanging on is futile.

Courage can patiently wait for contentment to rise without forcing a demanded state of well-being.

Courage grasps on to the reverence for life and does not let go of the idea and practice. Ever.

Our Obligation

"Reverence for life" was an ethic offered to the world more than a hundred years ago by Dr. Albert Schweitzer.

For Dr. Schweitzer, reverence was the imperative for how we should respect and positively affirm the world and all life.

Deepening this imperative, reverence for life certainly obligates us to reverence for our human story.

In reverence for the human story, lies the possibility for us all to fulfill the promise of our life and lives together.

In reverence for our human story—

We must resurrect desires as a force for good in our lives.

We must search for fulfillment in the spirit of the common good and not just for self-interest.

We must live with loss as a wound to heal and hold, not as a scar to hide or worse, as anger that is used against others so they will lose too.

We must work through our anxiety with healing activity and growth.

We must allow our courage to guide our steps toward desire and contentment, saving us from the harsh reality of the suffering soul.

We must see diversity in a new way; we must see our different expressions as an outpouring of the common depth and breadth of humanity.

In reverence for our human story—

Governments must lead and legislate as humans for humans, in sacred trust of our shared story and our deepest desires.

Societies and communities must not exist in isolation but seek to connect around our human story and let this be the basis by which we grow globally and for the common good.

Religion must reclaim our humanity and inspire a vision of the human soul as good. Then, worship and adherence to doctrine can be directed toward the loftiness of who we are and away from our continual denouncement and doom.

Educators must enlighten the story of our humanity. Knowledge cannot end with stored facts, but must promote exploration and curiosity and the deepening of our experience.

Professional caregivers must consider the whole human and make assessments of need and intervene from the fullness of human living, suffering and dying.

The family, however assembled together in number and kind, must be the cradle of care

for our human story and nurture its future
with love and respect.

All palaces, organizations and people that
hold real and perceived power must be the
guardians of the human story, protect it from
harm and enhance it for the good.

In reverence for our human story—

We must view health, in all its forms, as
necessary for human vitality.

We must view vitality as sacred for all and
seek ways to ensure its presence in each life.

We must strive to protect all vital sources of
life for they offer us the promise of a future
story.

And so it goes for the earth--we should not
seek to destroy this earth for the mere sake of
gaining more, but see the earth's life as life
amid all other life, worthy of reverence.

And so it goes for each other--we should lay down our weapons and *"beat our swords into ploughshares"* and work as diligently as we can to lift up our human story.

And so it goes for our dialogue with each other, it should not be destroyed by cheap networks of connection, but rather strive for the personal and real.

In reverence for our human story—

We can extend grace to each other, for while our lives are beautiful they are also complicated.

We can extend forgiveness because in the complications of life mistakes and madness is born.

We can extend hospitality for we are humans in need of each other.

We can extend understanding as we embrace the story we share.

For the sake of all we love,

For the hope of a quality of life and better future,

For the human story we all live,

We must strive now toward a reverence for our human story.

***

The lamp is lit.
Darkness backs up,
but only a bit.
So we are here,
in light's warm glow,
what will we do?
Be afraid of the dark still there?
Worry about the light's staying power?
No, we look into the heart of our humanity,
blessed communion,
that holds us together.

Last Words

There have been many moments in human history when old ways have not served and new ways and ideas must be born to meet the challenges of the present moment.

We are at such a moment.

If it is a given that we have a common human story.

If it is a given that this common human story has been hurt by our insistence on labeling and dividing humanity into a million categories and forever keeping us strangers.

If it is a given the forces are great to keep the division of humanity ever present.

If it is a given this division has given rise to terrible trends and events to use power as a means to control, even destroy, others not of the same group or people.

If it is a given that in today's news these tendencies toward power and control go unfettered, even with our best efforts toward diversity and sensitivity training.

Then, surely it must be a given at this moment we need a new way of imagining ourselves together on this planet.

The old sacred text says, *"Come now, let us reason together."*

Let us reason together for the purpose of understanding our problems at their most fundamental and basic causes.

Let us reason together in order to stop the damage of dividing humanity into complex categories that leads to costly and painful errors in understanding.

Let us reason together in order to stop using our misunderstanding as the means to propagate abuse, neglect and violence against others.

Let us reason together for in the effort of reason comes wisdom.

With wisdom comes a different way of being and living among each other.

With wisdom comes understanding of our human story, the heart of our humanity.

About the Author

I have worked for 22 years among humanity in a leadership and caregiving capacity as a spiritual, emotional and clinical ethics counselor in the critical and complex setting of the hospital.

In the hospital, I have been witness to and part of helping others sort through some of life's most difficult issues that produce some of life's most perplexing questions.

In my own personal journey, I have lived as a contemplative, pondering over the meaning of human existence. As a result, I have been through some profound experiences at great cost to me and others, and some of great joy, but all of great value.

I am flawed. Yet, over the years, a kind of self-care has set in and I have found comfort in letting elements of the lower graces and places take care of me.

My life is full.

I am the father of two sons and their lives matter most to me.

I am fortunate to enjoy the good and simple things of life.

I am aware that the wounds of the body and soul I carry complicate life for me but they also make me whole.

I am rich with family, friends and loves that are lasting.

I am indeed content to be my very human self.

All the best to each of us as we live our humanity in these crucial days,

Mark

mark@propertyofhumanity.com